Class 37s in South Wales

Anybody interested in British diesels during the last 40 years or so would have surely come across the Class 37 in South Wales. These locos were allocated to Cardiff straight from the production line and four decades later, they can still be seen. From the days of the early BR green livery, to BR blue, then the colourful Railfreight years, the 37/7s, the 37/9s and in more recent times EWS 37/4s, there is no doubt the Class 37 has a huge place in Welsh railway history.

To mark 40 years of service this pictorial book takes a journey through South Wales, showing the various lines, the types of train, the different locomotives and their liveries. This is not supposed to be a history book, just a timely reminder of what a wonderful, resourceful and photogenic locomotive the Class 37 is.

As most books on South Wales seem to start at Severn Tunnel Junction and head west, I've decided to go in the other direction! In addition, I've split the book into two parts, firstly looking at freight trains west to east and then passenger services including the Rhymney line.

With Class 60s and 66s working most of the freight today, just a couple of Class 37s still remain in South Wales, exclusively for the Rhymney service. Whatever their future holds, there's no denying their illustrious history which I hope is relived and remembered in this volume.

I would like to thank Phil Wright, Jim Ramsay, Dave Higson, Pete Rogers, Tony Wilson and John Griffiths for the use of their slides and photographs. A special thank you is extended to John Hooson, not only for his excellent slides but also his knowledge of railways in South Wales. Finally I would like to thank Mary, Elizabeth, Jason and David for their help in the preparation and production of this book.

Enjoy the book
Nick Meskell
October 2006

ISBN 0-9548035-7-4   First Published 2006

Lower quadrant signals, HAA Coal Hoppers and a 'Heavyweight' Class 37 in Railfreight grey with Coal sub-sector branding - a typical scene from the early/mid 1990s with 37897 at Ystrad Mynach on 17th March 1992. *(Nick Meskell collection)*

NAMED CLASS 37s IN SOUTH WALES

A number of Class 37s were officially named during their years in South Wales and the table below gives details of each one. To avoid confusion, the table only shows nameplates relevant to Wales. For example, in 1992, 37239 was based at Cardiff Canton carrying the name 'The Coal Merchants' Association of Scotland'! Other out of place examples are 37099 'Clydebridge' and 37137 'Clyde Iron' which were also Canton based in 1993, while at the same time 37427 'Bont Y Bermo' was working off Thornaby and 37430 'Cwmbran' had made it all the way to Motherwell! In total, 31 Class 37s were named with a Welsh theme and some of these plates are still carried today:

Loco	Name	Date	Location
37180	'Sir Dyfed / County of Dyfed' (1)	28/05/81	Carmarthen Station
37220	'Westerleigh'	12/06/90	Westerleigh Oil Terminal, Bristol
37229	'The Cardiff Rod Mill' (2)	23/05/84	Cardiff Rod Mill
37402	'Bont Y Bermo' (3)	28/02/94	Crewe Diesel Depot
37411	'Ty Hafan'	01/06/97	Newport Station
37411	'Castell Caerffili / Caerphilly Castle' (4)	28/11/05	Caerphilly Station
37414	'Cathays C & W Works 1846 - 1993'	18/03/93	Cardiff Cathays C & W Works
37417	'Richard Trevithick'	21/02/04	Merthyr Tydfil Station
37422	'Cardiff Canton'	31/01/03	Cardiff Canton
37425	'Pride of the Valleys / Balchder Y Cymoedd'	28/11/05	Caerphilly Station
37426	'Y Lein Fach / Vale of Rheidol'	05/05/86	Aberystwyth Station
37427	'Bont Y Bermo' (3)	13/04/86	Barmouth Station
37428	'David Lloyd George'	16/05/87	Pwllheli Station
37429	'Sir Dyfed / County of Dyfed' (1)	02/04/87	Cardiff Canton
37429	'Eisteddfod Genedlaethol'	05/08/87	Portmadoc Station
37430	'Cwmbran'	11/05/86	Cwmbran Station
37431	'Sir Powys / County of Powys'	17/06/87	Llandrindod Wells Station
37698	'Coed Bach'	21/09/88	Coed Bach Washery
37702	'Taff Merthyr'	20/11/89	Cardiff Canton
37711	'Tremorfa Steelworks'	09/11/88	Cardiff Tidal Sidings
37712	'The Cardiff Rod Mill' (2)	09/11/88	Cardiff Tidal Sidings
37799	'Sir Dyfed / County of Dyfed' (1)	07/11/87	Cardiff Canton
37800	'Glo Cymru'	27/09/86	Aberthaw Power Station
37801	'Aberthaw / Aberddawan'	27/09/86	Aberthaw Power Station
37886	'Sir Dyfed / County of Dyfed' (1)	c July 2001	Cardiff Canton
37887	'Castell Caerffili / Caerphilly Castle' (4)	c Sep 1992	Cardiff Canton
37898	'Cwmbargoed DP' (5)	20/04/93	Cwm Bargoed Disposal Point
37899	'Sir Gorllewin Morgannwg / County of West Glamorgan'	01/05/91	Neath Station
37901	'Mirrlees Pioneer'	03/12/86	Cardiff Canton
37902	'British Steel Llanwern'	05/06/91	Llanwern
37905	'Vulcan Enterprise'	03/02/87	Cardiff Canton

(1) The nameplates 'Sir Dyfed / County of Dyfed' were carried by 37180 between May 1981 and January 1987. 37429 received them in April 1987 but carried them for only three months. 37799 was next, receiving them in November 1987 and carrying them right through until May 2001. By a twist of fate, 37180, now renumbered as 37886, had them refitted in June/July 2001 after a gap of 14 years!

(2) 37229 was first with 'The Cardiff Rod Mill' plates which were carried from May 1984 until July/August 1988.

(3) 37427 was first with 'Bont Y Bermo' plates which were carried from April 1986 until April 1993.

(4) The nameplates 'Castell Caerffili / Caerphilly Castle' were carried by 37887 from August or September 1992. A GWR style of the nameplates are carried by 37411. This name has also been carried by 47615 and 47727.

(5) The nameplates on 37898 are incorrectly spelt!

It is worth recording that 37675 has carried the unofficial painted name of 'Margam TMD' since 2001.

FREIGHT TRAINS

Trainload Petroleum and Trainload Coal branding paired together with 37889 and 37689 near Kidwelly on 22nd April 1991 working 6V07, the 07.45 from Ellesmere Port Cawoods to Coed Bach Washery. With the flat sands stretching for miles along the South Wales coast, it was thought the Germans might use this area for an assault during World War 2. To prevent such action, reinforced concrete blocks designed to obstruct the progress of a tank or armoured vehicle were sited here and 50 years on, they remained in place, mostly used these days by sheep! This train was not normally double-headed and on this day it was routed via the main line due to a problem on the Swansea avoiding line. The extra loco would certainly have been useful on the 1 in 52 gradient of Cockett Bank. Coed Bach Opencast Coal Disposal Point closed in March 1998 thus ending this colourful North West - South Wales flow. Both 37s here were based at Canton in April 1991. *(John Hooson)*

Opposite: Diverging from Neath and at Brecon Junction are two freight only lines to Onllwyn and Cwmgwrach. The latter terminus is seen here in all its glory with the first six hoppers loaded behind 37701 on 13th April 1994. At this time there were two trains a day from this location, 6C11, the 05.20 Aberthaw to Cwmgwrach empties which arrived at 07.22, returning as 7C11 at 08.55 and 6C17, the 10.15 also from Aberthaw, which arrived at 12.49 and departed as 7C17, the 14.20 back to Aberthaw. 37701 worked off Canton from June 1986 until November 1998. Today, wearing 'Transrail' livery, this loco is dumped at Old Oak Common, having not run in service this century! *(Dave Higson)*

Above: A very industrial setting on the four-track main line between Port Talbot Station and Margam with 37294 heading east with a rake of TUA chemical tanks from Baglan Bay on 21st April 1989. Allocated to Cardiff Canton when built, 37294 enjoyed a distinguished career in South Wales with stints at Cardiff in the 1970s and all of the 1980s in between moves to Landore, Eastfield, Inverness and Motherwell. In August 1999 the loco was exported to France where it worked for a year before a return to the UK and autumnal 'sandite' duties. The loco last ran in December 2003 and is presently stored at Crewe wearing the Civil Engineers 'Dutch' livery. *(John Hooson)*

Below: A matching pair of Trainload Metal branded locos in the shape of 37716 and 37886 on 6B52, the 14.58 from Llanwern to Port Talbot Docks pictured near Margam on 20th April 1989. The wagons here are 100 ton tipplers (code PTA), returning empty to be loaded with imported iron ore. For several years, the fully loaded train with 33 wagons in tow was the heaviest on the BR system, weighing in at a staggering 3300 tons! Initially the motive power was 3 x 37/0s, then 2 x 56s, then 2 x 37/7s and finally a single Class 60. There were normally 5 trains in each direction each day.
(John Hooson)

Opposite: Same day and same location with BR blue 37223 working 6A35, the 17.45 Pantyffynnon to Didcot. In the mid 1980s, the Domestic Coal business was reorganised and the 'Speedlink Coal Network' (SCN) was born. The wagons pictured are 60mph HEAs and although destined for Didcot, this was only an intermediate point. From there the coal would go to the Coal Concentration Depots (CCD) in London at West Drayton or Neasden or to various smaller CCDs in the south of England. Despite being sold to DRS for main line use in 2001 and moved to Brush at Loughborough for overhaul, the work was cancelled and 37223 was broken for scrap in 2003. *(John Hooson)*

Below: Inside Margam depot with 37078 and another BR blue 37/0 sometime in the late 1980s. Although used for maintenance purposes, Class 37s were not based here until recent years and this only came about following the closure of Canton. With its large and out of position numerals 37078 was never really a Welsh locomotive, spending many years at Gateshead, March and Thornaby. It was named 'Teesside Steelmaster' in 1984. Between May 1988 and January 1993 this loco (now nameless) worked off Canton until a move to Inverness and the prestigious Inter City IISA pool! Withdrawn in December 1993, the loco was finally scrapped in February 2004. *(Travel Lens Photographic)*

Opposite: 37692 passes Tondu signal box on 28th September 1990 with 7B65, the 09.20 from Llynfi Junction, one of the many 'last trains' from Maesteg. The driver hands the token to signaller Selwyn Blyth. During this period, there were no passenger services to Maesteg. The station closed in July 1970 and was reopened in September 1992. Today, there is a train every hour, with a journey time of 55 minutes through to Cardiff. 37692 is another lesser known Cardiff machine, only working in South Wales between 1987 and 1990. Based at Motherwell in September 1993, the loco was named 'The Lass O' Ballochmyle' in a ceremony at Ayr TMD. *(John Hooson)*

Above: Taken in the same location as the previous image, but this time showing the full extent of the huge signal box. This is 37796 heading from the Maesteg line again on 29th July 1992. The junction here splits three ways. The line to Ogmore Vale closed in 1989 and is now lifted, the Llynfi Valley branch to Maesteg, as already mentioned, reopened to passengers in 1992, while the line to the right, to Pontycymmer closed to passengers in 1953 but survived as a freight branch for many years. Presently mothballed, it was reopened between 1991 and 1997 to carry one million tons of screened coal from tips in the valley as part of a land reclamation scheme. In the photo, 37796 also exchanges the single line token and the signal box remains in use today. Coal branded 37796 is now stored at Tyne Yard in the WZKF pool which, along with seven other 37/7s, is a pool of 'possible hire locomotives to France'!
(Nick Meskell collection)

Opposite: A third image from this area and here comes 37802 heading towards one of the reclamation sites in October 1996. There were three Class 37 hauled trains per week in the autumn of 1996, running as 6Z60, the 13.10 TThSO Aberthaw to Pontycymmer, returning as 7Z60, the 16.53 TThSO back to Aberthaw. Originally formed in 1988, the Bridgend Valley Railway Company gained permission in 2001 from Railtrack and the Welsh Assembly to reopen a four mile stretch of line between Pontycymmer and Caegarw. At Pontycymmer, an engine shed and workshop have been built so far. The picture opposite is somewhat typical of this line and judging by the exhaust smoke, 37802 is working hard around the sharp curves, through the trees and along the valley floor. Exported to Spain in 2001 and numbered L32, this former Welsh beast was involved in a severe accident near Catalayud in January 2003 and was scrapped six months later. *(Dave Higson)*

Below: Back to the main line at Brynna, between Cardiff and Bridgend, and another image of 6V07, heading for Coed Bach. The date here is 27th September 1990. Train loco is 37894, formerly 37124, an Eastfield loco in the early/mid 1980s and another ex-Welsh 37/7 to work in France. A total of 172 container flats were built between 1986 and 1988 to carry these colourful Cawood coal containers. Given a TOPS code of PFA these containers conveyed coal destined for Ireland. *(John Hooson)*

Opposite: As already recorded, early Welsh 37s were normally of the centre headcode design but during the sectorisation years, lower numbered locos were transferred in, like 37109 opposite. From the mid-1970s, this loco was moved countrywide, enjoying stints at Thornaby, March, Tinsley, Motherwell, Inverness, Cardiff, Bristol, Stratford, Eastleigh, Toton and Crewe! During its Cardiff years, the loco rounds the curve at Miskin on 3rd March 1993, with 8B51, the 10.35 Llandeilo Junction to Alexandra Dock engineers train. Complete with a brake van in the middle, these are ZFV 'Dogfish' two-axle ballast hoppers with side and centre chutes. *(John Hooson)*

Above: With buffer beam skirts and circular buffers 37244 basks in the low winter sunshine at Radyr yard on Sunday 29th January 1978. Looking at the picture in detail and this is what a true Welsh Class 37 looked like or if you had to describe a Canton-based BR blue 37/0 from the 1970s, then here it is. Delivered as new to Cardiff in September 1964 as D6944, this loco dodged reallocation, conversion and renumbering and spent a staggering 26 years allocated to either Canton or Landore, mostly Canton. During that period the loco would have worked just about every type of train South Wales had to offer and from BR green to BR blue, came Railfreight Distribution, Civil Engineers and two tone grey. Moving from Cardiff to Immingham in October 1990, 37244 also worked off Stratford, Tinsley and Toton before withdrawal and a move to Springs Branch depot in Wigan for cutting in February 1999. *(Nick Meskell collection)*

Opposite below: A powerful shot of 37254 heading south through Radyr with a fully loaded coal train from Tower on 25th June 1986. The junction at Radyr splits two ways sending trains to Cardiff Central via Cathays and then westbound or directly via Canton depot to Cardiff Central and eastbound towards Newport. Eight miles north of Radyr is Pontypridd where the line splits for Treherbert and Aberdare/Merthyr Tydfil. Beyond Aberdare is the famous Tower Colliery. Opened in 1878, more than 1000 were employed post-World War 2. In 1994, British Coal closed the colliery because they thought it would be uneconomical. They were proved wrong after a successful buy-out by the workforce produced 450,000 tons of anthracite in 1995, making over £4million profit! Anthracite is a pure mineral coal which emits few hydrocarbons and burns almost without smoke! This colliery is now the only deep mine left in Wales. *(Nick Meskell collection)*

Below: A trio of BR blue locos rest between duties at Radyr yard on Saturday 21st June 1986. Nearest the camera is 37254 coupled to 37233 with 37231 at the back. At the time, this image was somewhat typical for South Wales with these 21-year old Bristol and Cardiff based unrefurbished 37/0s working together. 37254 dodged the refurbishment programme and survived in service until November 1998. It was purchased privately in March 2003 and is presently undergoing restoration in Kent. 37233 became 37889 and is presently stored at Crewe, having last run in June 1999. 37231 clings onto its Welsh history and is presently stored at Margam, having last run in January 2005, numbered 37896. *(Nick Meskell collection)*

The first of two images taken from the famous footbridge opposite Cardiff Canton depot and this is 20th June 1986 with 37293 and a rake of 14 two-axle chemical tanks heading east. Also pictured on page seven, this flow originated from BP Chemicals' terminal at Baglan Bay and ran through to Hull. The year 1986 may have been a turning point in the history of the Welsh Class 37. With numerous locos swallowed up in the 37/4 programme, even more locos were passing through the works and emerging as 37/5s, 37/7s and 37/9s. New liveries were on their way and the days of the original and now 20+ year old 37/0s in BR Blue were numbered. In the summer of 1986, Cardiff had an allocation of 79 Class 37s, consisting of 44 x 37/0s, 6 x 37/4s, 18 x 37/5s, 8 x 37/7s and 3 x 37/9s. Looking at the batch of 37/0s in particular and all of them were now fitted with train air brakes, a good number had additional fuel capacity while three locos, 37181, 37186 and 37187 still retained steam heat boilers although all of them were isolated! 37293 pictured, the former D6993, was another diehard Welsh machine, allocated to Canton from new in July 1965 until transfer to Motherwell in September 1990. It returned to Canton in May 1992, staying for a year and in July 1999 it travelled through the Channel Tunnel for a new life in France. Returning to the UK in August 2000, the loco was towed to Tyne Yard. Six years on, the loco still resides at this location painted in the attractive BR Mainline Freight livery of aircraft blue with a silver stripe. *(Nick Meskell collection)*

From the initial batch of 31 Class 37/4 locomotives, South Wales received an allocation of six machines, the last six of those converted, namely 37426 to 37431. These locos were supplied for services on the Cambrian lines and included runs to Aberystwyth and Pwllheli (with through trains to/from London Euston). There was a bizarre evening turn from Carmarthen to Milford Haven and back in summer 1986. The train was 2B98, the 17.10 from Swansea which was worked by a 47/4 from Swansea to Carmarthen before the 37/4 took over. The train returned as 1C82, the 19.30 to Bristol Temple Meads which employed the same 37/4 back to Carmarthen, the same 47/4 back to Swansea for a different 47/4 to Bristol on weekdays and amazingly a Class 50 on Saturdays! (Three different locos booked on one journey of 158 miles). Another Cardiff 37/4 turn was 1V01, the 02.04 MO Crewe to Cardiff. In later years these locos became common between Liverpool/Manchester and Cardiff vice 'Sprinter' DMUs. Things became rather odd in the 1990s when for example, 37427 'Bont Y Bermo' ended up at Inverness in Scotrail branded Regional Railways livery while 37422 moved from the Highlands to South Wales, also gaining a coat of RR! In the photo 37422 passes the disused goods yard opposite Canton with an engineers train, probably bound for Alexandra Dock Junction on 28th August 1999. Taken 13 years apart, little has changed between the two images except for the trees and bushes. *(Jim Ramsay)*

Two pictures taken in Canton yard itself and here is 37801, the new order of Railfreight Class 37 for South Wales in the mid-1980s. As part of a life extension programme, a total of 43 Class 37/0s were overhauled as 37/7s and were numbered between 37701 and 37899. The numbering system was a little odd as it was clearly designed to accomodate 200 examples, but only these numbers were actually used: 37701 to 37719, 37797 to 37803 and 37883 to 37899. To confuse matters further, 37801 was not a 37/8, it was a 37/7 and like its sisters, the main generator was replaced with an alternator, regeared bogies were fitted and ballast weights were added increasing the total weight by about 12-15 tons to 120 tons which resulted in the nickname 'Heavyweights'. The new Railfreight grey with a large BR sign became the standard livery. In the photo 37801 somewhat typifies the new dawn of 1980s Railfreight. Looking neat and tidy with red buffer beams and its 'Aberddawan / Aberthaw' nameplates (see page 4), this loco worked off Canton between 1986 and 1993 before further moves to Immingham, Motherwell, Toton and Crewe. In July 2001, 37801 emigrated to warmer shores, starting a new life as L29 in Spain, painted in GIF livery. Along with eleven other 37/7s, many of which were once based at Cardiff, the loco is still listed as operational. Originally fourteen 37/7s were hired to GIF in Spain to help with the construction of the new high speed line between Lleida and Tarragona / Barcelona. Formerly D6873, then 37173 and built at the English Electric factory in Newton-Le-Willows, this loco is 43 years old at the time of writing. *(Travel Lens Photographic)*

A powerful zoom shot from the aforementioned footbridge at Canton with five Class 37/0s stabled on 25th June 1986. Left to right at the front we have 37187 with buffer beam skirts, circular buffers, miniature snowploughs and a 'domino' headcode box; 37298 with the slightly revised front end look, oval buffers and sealed yellow headcode box and 37236 looking awesome with a dropped domino spot, circular buffers and skirts. Further scrutiny of the image reveals further minor differences such as lamp brackets and grab rails. This was a regular stabling point for 37s, more so on weekends when coal production was not as high hence less trains and spare locos. Note the oil saturated track, almost void of ballast!
(Nick Meskell collection)

The first of four images at Cardiff Central Station and away from the more picturesque locations in Wales, half a day on this station would provide a feast of loaded and empty coal train movements with maybe 20 different 37s in a seven or eight hour period. Starting with 37294 and 37223 and an eastbound Merry-Go-Round (HAA) train from 1986 passing through platform 7. Merry-Go-Round trains started in the 1960s and were a highly efficient way of moving coal using semi-permanently coupled sets. These air braked, high capacity wagons automatically loaded and unloaded coal in a non-stop operation and although investment in modern loading/unloading techniques did not take place at some collieries, HAAs were still being used, working with the traditional methods of tractors and JCBs. 37294, the former D6994, was another Welsh stalwart. Delivered new to Canton in 1965, the loco had an unbroken spell in South Wales that lasted a staggering 27 years! It was 1991 before a transfer to Eastfield took place, then Inverness and Motherwell. Like others featured so far, the loco worked in France in 1999/2000 and after a return to the UK and a period of storage, the loco was transferred to.... Cardiff Canton! Now in its 41st year and surviving today in store at Crewe, this loco has never been based at an English depot! 37223 is already pictured on page 8 and together with its sister, provides a total of 3500hp to haul this train. With the Blue Star multiple working method, one driver powers both locos although sometimes the second (or third) loco is manned for safety reasons. Both 37s pictured here were in the FQLC pool in 1986, which was basically 'Coal Distribution Class 37 pool'. *(Nick Meskell collection)*

Same day, same direction and 37303 passes through the centre roads with a fully loaded rake of MDV mineral wagons. Between 1961 and 1963, nearly 5000 of these two-axle vacuum braked wagons were built by BR. They featured two side doors and an end door and were common in South Wales right from the start of Class 37 traction. Wearing a simple coat of BR Blue 37303 retains circular buffers but the skirts have been removed. This locomotive had a interesting history, not so much for livery, namings or allocation but different fleet numbers. Originally D6603, it was in amongst the last batch of Class 37 locomotives built at Newton-Le-Willows in 1965 and it moved straight to 87E (Landore) upon completion. Switching between Landore and Canton, in 1974 it became 37303 under TOPS. With 37300 converted to 37429, 37301 to 37412 and 37302 to 37416, a 37/4 conversion looked likely for this machine. Instead, it avoided any kind of major work and in 1989, was renumbered 37271. By this time, the original 37271 had become 37418! (37s 304, 306 and 308 became 37 272, 273 and 274 at the same time). (Are you confused yet?). This new number lasted until 1994, when it became 37333 as a member of the new 37/3 sub-class! The loco (carrying whatever number) survived for many years until it was involved in an accident at Rotherham Steel Terminal in 1995 led to its untimely demise. It was withdrawn then stored at Crewe for two years before being scrapped. *(Nick Meskell collection)*

Staying in June 1986 and a third BR blue Class 37 hauled coal train passes Central Station. Routed along platform 6, this is 37158 with a rake of empty HAA hoppers heading west. Unlike many 37s which were swapped between operating pools and depots from the mid-1980s onwards, this machine moved frequently in the early years and after delivery to 87E (Landore) in 1963, the loco moved to 64B (Haymarket) in 1966 and then 65A (Eastfield). Returning to South Wales and Cardiff in 1972, it was moved to Bristol in 1980 and, if records are correct, was working off March depot when this image was taken. After a fire in 1999, the loco was withdrawn and then purchased for preservation in 2000 by Type 3 Traction. Following a move to the West Coast Railway Company's depot at Carnforth, restoration work began but a swap deal saw 37158 become part of the WCRC fleet while 37248 was acquired by Type 3 Traction. Today, this loco is stored. *(Nick Meskell collection)*

37799 'Sir Dyfed / County of Dyfed' enters Cardiff Central Station with a loaded train of MGRs bound for Aberthaw on 5th May 1989. There was something exceptionally insensitive about the conversion of split box headcode 37s into this flat fronted bland look. Although worse was to come for certain DRS locomotives which lost all nose end features, the pleasing split box with yellow or black glass/panelling and centre connecting door certainly gave the locomotive a bit of character. A book may well be written about the Class 37 numbering schemes from the 1980s onwards and this machine was a classic victim. From a simple 37061, the loco was allocated 37501 when undergoing overhaul in the early spring of 1986. 37005 took up this dubious honour instead, leaving 37061 to become 37599, a number it actually received! Then, common sense (!) and, 37799! Summer 1989 was an interesting one at Canton. There was the DCWA pool which contained 37/0s for Civil Engineers; the FQLC pool (Coal Distribution) which had more 37/0s and the FAWC pool (Aggregates) for yet more 37/0s. There were two 37/3s in the FPLW pool (Petroleum). There were eleven 37/7s in the FHCC pool (General Coal); the FECA pool (Power Station Coal) was made up of 37/7s (including 37799); the FMCH pool (Metals) consisted of more 37/7s; the FMCC pool (Metals) was dedicated to 37/9s and finally, the PXXA pool (Provincial Services) which consisted of the six 37/4s. (Why so many pools?). Liveries included BR blue, Railfreight, Red stripe Railfreight, Large Logo, grey with various sub sector markings and odd liveries like 37350 in BR green, 37146 in Large Logo but with a small logo (!) and 37693, pictured on page 32 in Railfreight grey and large numbers!
(Nick Meskell collection)

Opposite: Heading out of surburbia and into the valleys and a stunning image of 37689. Long before Class 37 hauled passenger trains ran to Rhymney, the growl of the 37 could be heard on the freight only branch from Ystrad Mynach which served three collieries plus the opencast at Cwm Bargoed and the rather splendidly named 'Nelson Bog' shale disposal point. The train here is 6A81, the 09.50 from Nelson Sidings to Taff Merthyr on 2nd March 1990. With Ocean Colliery winding gear in the background, this empty MGR train is on its way to Taff Merthyr Colliery, just a mile or so further on. Opened in 1924, this colliery employed an incredible 1600 men in the early 1930s and 735 in the 1970s. It closed in October 1992. *(John Hooson)*

Above: Relatively small amounts of coal were being loaded at Cwm Bargoed in the late 1980s, but following the re-opening of the British Coal Disposal Point in September 1990, services gradually built up to about three a day including Sundays. 37796 and 37701 carefully bring coal down the steeply graded branch (much of it at 1 in 40) from Cwm Bargoed and are shown high above the valley floor, where Taff Merthyr and Trelewis Pits can just be glimpsed. The train is 7C90, the 17.16 Cwm Bargoed to Aberthaw on 16th April 1991. Phil Mackay, a driver from Barry, used to carry his train reporting numbers in his bag and would display them on any trains he drove. He's obviously on this one! *(John Hooson)*

Below: There is something very pleasing about a pair of coal branded 37s working a fully loaded train of HAA coal hoppers on a fine sunny day and here is a perfect example, near Cwn Bargoed, with 37803 and 37699 on 16th April 1991. The train is 7C79, 08.24 Cwm Bargoed to Aberthaw. This line went through various phases of using single and pairs of Class 37s but with severe gradients, steepening to 1 in 35/36 in places, it was deemed more appropriate to use pairs. In the photo this pair cautiously work their 28 wagon train down the grade. Cwm Bargoed Disposal Point itself has been mothballed for some years now, but the operators are looking to appeal the overturning of Welsh Assembly permission, denied by the High Court, at appeal in October 2006. If successful, there will be another ten million tons of coal making its way down the valley. *(John Hooson)*

Opposite: Having joined the main Rhymney Cardiff Line at Ystrad Mynach, 37797 and 37887 accelerate away down the valley after delivering to the signalman the single line token which controlled the section to/from Cwm Bargoed. On Sundays at this time engineers possessions meant closure of the line towards Cardiff until lunch time forcing two loaded trains to wait at Cwm Bargoed ready to come down. Once this first train passed through the section, the second was released immediately. This was the first train on 26th February 1995, 7C35, the 14.10 to Aberthaw. Once again, both locos carry coal branding. Today, a photographer would struggle to find a Class 37 hauled train anywhere in Britain on a Sunday, whereas a decade ago there were two on the same line within one hour! *(John Hooson)*

Continuing west and moving on to steel trains with 37713 on the freight only line to Ebbw Vale on 29th October 1988. Pictured at Waunlwyd this was a 'Z' working from Waunlwyd to Margam. Before the new yards were built a mile or so nearer to Ebbw Vale, trains would arrive at, and depart from, Waunlwyd, zig-zagging their way up three levels to where the British Steel Corporation locos would take over for the final mile into the works. Waunlwyd Yards were closed and the lines lifted in January 1989 to make way for preparations for the 1992 Garden Festival site. This train was unusual for a Saturday, but there had been an urgent call from Ravenscraig Steelworks at Motherwell for empty wagons to load more steel coils bound for either Shotton or Cardiff/Margam in South Wales. *(John Hooson)*

Staying on the Ebbw Vale line and a smart looking 37905 'Vulcan Enterprise' at Llanhilleth on 31st October 1988 working 6B88, the 10.30 Llanwern to Waunlwyd. *(John Hooson)*

Arrival at Newport with the odd looking 37693! As well as a bizarre numbering system, the refurbished 37s also acquired some unusual liveries and although 37693 is in Railfreight grey with a Large Logo, the unusually large and out of position fleet numbers add a different twist. Under the new skin, this is 37210 which was one of a few locomotives which started its days in South Wales and duly returned after overhaul and conversion. In 1990 it moved from Canton to Eastfield and the FEPE pool hauling Scottish power station coal alongside a few other 37/5s, three 37/3s and four 26/0s. The loco lost this colourful coat for two tone grey with sub sector branding. On 23rd March 1990, the loco was named 'Sir William Arrol' in a ceremony at Edinburgh Waverley. When researching these Welsh Class 37 histories, there is rarely a happy ending and in this case 37693 is dumped at Tyne Yard having last run in October 2000. *(Nick Meskell collection)*

Left: 37901 'Mirrlees Pioneer' heads out of Highfield Tunnels and into Newport Station with a loaded steel train on 30th August 1996. The six strong class of 37/9 were all converted from 37/0s in 1986/1987. All were fitted with prototype power units and ballast weights and 901 to 904 received a Mirrlees engine and Brush alternator while 905 and 906 got a Ruston engine and a GEC alternator. They may well have still looked like 37s, but they made a completely new noise! The 37/9s worked dedicated out and back diagrams from South Wales and they were only ever based at Canton. Privatisation in the late 1990s saw the abandonment of this experiment. Like any small class, they were expensive to maintain and regarded as non-standard. 37901 worked for 12 years before a period of store, then preservation. Today, restored to a very high standard, the loco can be found working between Llangollen and Carrog on the seven mile long Llangollen Railway. *(Nick Meskell collection)*

Right: Passing through the small platform at Newport on 20th June 1985 is a grimy 37235 in BR blue. Although passing freights could be routed along any platform or the centre roads, they were often put over this far side if a crew change was forthcoming or another freight / passenger train was scheduled to pass. While on this platform, the train blocked access to Godfrey Road sidings, so they didn't normally wait too long. 37235 was named 'The Coal Merchants Association of Scotland' in November 1987 at Aberdeen. Oddly, it was still based at Canton at this time! The plates were removed in March 1991 and fitted to 37239. *(Nick Meskell collection)*

Below: Moving across to Holland, well, Godfrey Road sidings at Newport actually with an incredible line up of no less than five 37/0s all wearing the Civil Engineers 'Dutch' livery! 37230 is nearest the camera in this 23rd July 1993 image. These sidings at Newport were used extensively by Class 37s for many years. Now lifted as part of a redevelopment, the 37s would stable in between duties with Newport being used as a signing on point for train crews. It's probably safe to say that at any time from the mid-1960s until 2004/2005 there would have been at least one Class 37 stabled, but not any more. At this time in 1993, there were about 50 Class 37/0s and a few 37/3s painted in this grey and yellow colour scheme. The locos here were in either the Canton based REJK or IGJK pools, which basically covered Inter City Infrastructure on the Great Western main line or general Infrastructure work in South Wales and West. Among the locos allocated were 37012, the former 'Loch Rannoch' and other Scottish celebrities, 37263 and 37264. Reference is made again to the rarity of getting five 37s in identical liveries together. This really is a once in a lifetime opportunity. It was a Friday so perhaps they were being gathered for weekend engineering work but no 56s or 60s - very lucky! *(Jim Ramsay)*

Opposite: Just out of Newport and across the River Usk is Maindee West Junction, which splits north and east. Northbound trains head for Cwmbran, Abergavenny and Hereford while eastbound services pass East Usk Yard then head for Severn Tunnel Junction, Chepstow and Swindon. Just after this yard is East Usk Junction where this fine image of 37372 was taken. At this point a freight only line branches off to the right while the train is on the main line with a short ballast working from Tidenham to Alexandra Dock. The date is 2nd March 1990 and the headcode is 8B47. The 37/3s were an odd sub-class, made up of unrefurbished 37/0s with regeared bogies. They were, if you like, a poor man's 37/5. A total of 18 examples were running in 1990, numbered pretty randomly between 37350 and 37381. Many of them reverted back to their old identities in later years. 37372, formerly 37159, was working in the Canton based DCWA pool in 1990. This was a departmental pool for the Western Region Civil Engineer. Withdrawn in December 2004, this loco is now stored at Motherwell and painted in the blue Mainline livery. *(John Hooson)*

Opposite: Between Newport and Severn Tunnel Junction is the impressive Llanwern Steel and Ironworks. Although the ironworks closed in 2001, half of the original works remains in production. The loss of iron ore trains closed one chapter but today the rail link is in constant use, with incoming trains moving steel slabs to be processed. Data from 2004 reveals over 50,000 tons of rolled steel were being produced each week. Pictured on the main line near the Llanwern site itself, comes an old school iron ore train with near original condition BR blue 37258 at the helm. The date here is 5th August 1981.
(Dave Higson)

Above: The final freight in our epic journey shows 37010 with a ballast train at Severn Tunnel Junction on 20th July 1993. As recorded on page 34, these 'Dutch' 37s were employed by the Civil Engineer and given their age and unrefurbished condition, hauling ballast and other permanent way trains around their area was pretty much all they did. Despite being dumped at Wigan waiting for cutting for many years, 37010 was one of nine 37s recently rescued by the Harry Needle Railroad Company for possible restoration, the other eight being 37100, 37131, 37170, 37178, 37667, 37672, 37680 and 37898.
(Nick Meskell collection)

PASSENGER TRAINS

The Large Logo 37/4 became a common sight in South Wales in the mid/late 1980s. Although the six locomotives were initially for Cambrian Coast services, they were soon drafted in to help on the Welsh Marches after the new Class 153 DMUs proved unreliable. There were two diagrams, Mondays to Saturdays, both out and back from Cardiff and both at very similiar times. In fact, they were ideal for photographers! The Liverpool Lime Street diagram started off at 05.07 with 1M06 to Liverpool, returning as 1V08, the 09.15 to Cardiff. The afternoon leg was 1M17, 13.23 to Liverpool, returning as 1V17, 17.14 to Cardiff. The Manchester Piccadilly diagram started out from Cardiff 43 minutes later with 1M08, the 05.50 northbound, returning as 1V09, 10.00 to Cardiff. The afternoon trip was again 40-odd minutes behind the Liverpool train, departing Cardiff Central at 14.00 (1M78) and finishing with 1V18, the 18.17 ex-Manchester. The stock used was normally four mark 2A air braked vehicles although mark 1 vacuum braked stock and an extra coach or two were often substituted. In the photo above, 37429 'Eisteddfod Genedlaethol' calls at Newport working one of the above trains in 1988. Although Class 37s had a long association with the Marches on both passenger and freight duties, this was a colourful interim period before the 1990s and frequent 37s on rugby and football specials. *(Nick Meskell collection)*

RAILTOURS

Left: Steep gradients, freight only branch lines and splendid scenery makes South Wales an ideal destination for railtours. This is 18th January 1992 during a photo-stop at Tenby with a painted up 37697 and 37412 at the front of the train heading, at this point, for Pembroke Dock. Named the 'Severn-Taff Cruncher', this quadruple 37 hauled train started from Gloucester and ran to Pembroke Dock, Whitland, Fishguard Harbour and Swansea before returning to Gloucester. The 697 digits over the headcode box were probably acceptable but 'LASH' (?), (noun), "a violent beating or impact". Was this a message to the driver? *(Nick Meskell collection)*

Right: The other end of the train, also at Tenby, with 37280 and 37137. Although all painted in grey, what are the odds of four locos with four different sub sectors all on the same train: 137 - Metals, 280 - Petroleum, 412 - Distribution and 697 - Coal! (Was this planned?). This train was organised by the Barry Open Day Committee and running as 1Z28 throughout, it was booked from Gloucester at 09.06 returning at 19.45, which wasn't such a lengthy day for just over 300 miles of tractor haulage. For the record, in January 1992, 37137 was named 'Clyde Iron' and was working in Cardiff's FMAK pool; 37280 was in the CF based FPEK pool; 37412 (ex-'Loch Lomond'), was based at Laira in the MDRL pool and 37697 was another Canton machine, but part of the FHBK pool. Although 37412 would become a regular on passenger trains around Cardiff in later years, it was clearly used on this day for its ETH supply and cleverly marshalled next to the stock! *(Nick Meskell collection)*

Apologies for another shot at Tondu but this railtour from 4th April 1992 was another Welsh classic. Organised by Pathfinder Tours, named 'The Hoove-Ring Druid' and running as 1Z16 throughout, this train started out from Manchester Piccadilly at 06.05 with 47574 which worked the train to Derby. From here the main motive power took over in the shape of 50033 and 50050. After a 30 minute layover at Cardiff and with 37212 now on the rear, the train continued through Bridgend, Tondu and on to the Pontycymmer branch. After a brief layover at Pontycymmer, it was the turn of 37212 to work the train and with a pair of 50s on the rear and 12 coaches in tow, it must have been an impressive ride! The photo shows 37212 at Tondu having worked the said journey in a recorded 34 minutes. (Tondu to Pontycymmer is just over five miles. The 50s took 28 minutes on the outward leg). From Tondu, 37212 worked forward to Margam where, after reversal, the 50s continued to Ebbw Vale. From here 37212 was in charge again, working the 19 mile journey to Newport. Here the 37 was detatched, the 50s returned to Derby and 47574 completed the day, working back to Manchester, arriving around 23.00. 37212 with its coal branding was based at Cardiff, working in the FQCK pool in April 1992. It moved to Scotland a month after this tour. *(Nick Meskell collection)*

RUGBY SPECIALS

Hosting international football, rugby league, rugby union, music concerts and motor sports, the Millennium Stadium in Cardiff is one of the most prestigious sports arenas in Britain today. Thanks to the redevelopment of Wembley Stadium in recent years, domestic English football finals have also been played at this venue and purely from an enthusiasts point of view, the late-1990s onwards have seen a plethora of locomotive hauled specials and service trains. From pairs of 31s, 33s and 37s, right through to a Class 46, numerous 47s and regular 67s, whenever there's a major sporting event at Cardiff, expect a train or two. Concentrating on the 37s and although not used anymore, there was a time when virtually all loco hauled services were worked by this class. This is the delightful location of Pontralis, with access to the timber terminal on the right of the picture. For a while, privately owned 37/0s, 37029, 37038 and 37197 were hired in for additional services and they often worked in pairs. This is Ian Riley owned 37197 in its unique livery on the 30th August 2003 with 1Z77, the 09.13 from Crewe to Cardiff. The same loco and stock returned north with 1M94, the 17.44 Cardiff to Crewe. *(Phil Wright)*

Below: Famous for its days in Scotland, then the Blackpool 'Club' trains, the North Wales line, the Rhymney line, chosen as one of three dedicated 37s for the Leeds - Carlisle service and a frequent performer on the Marches, here is 37408 'Loch Rannoch' at Pandy (near Abergavenny) also on 30th August 2003. This train was 1Z39, the 07.45 Crewe to Cardiff via Wrexham relief. The loco returned on 1Z34, the 18.15 Cardiff to Crewe, also via Wrexham. This was a pretty good day all round in South Wales with 37197 and 37408 working in from Crewe, 37410, 37417, 37422 and 37425 on the Rhymney services and 37886 working to Fishguard! *(Phil Wright)*

Opposite: A powerful shot of the beaten and bruised 37688 at Llanvihangel on 23rd August 2003 with 1Z33, the 07.45 Crewe to Cardiff via Wrexham. Although booked for ETH fitted locos, the odd no-heat example managed an appearance. These were hard times for EWS 37s. Once based at Tinsley and named 'Great Rocks' this loco had certainly fallen from grace by this time. Note the air horns, crudely removed from the roof and placed either side of the bonnet! The stock used in all three of these photos was owned by Riviera Trains and painted in their Oxford blue and cream livery. 'Felicity', 5373 is first behind the loco. This is a mark 2A, built in 1968. *(Phil Wright)*

CLASS 37s TO RHYMNEY

In 1995 a shortage of DMUs prompted a regular loco-hauled substitution between Cardiff and Rhymney. Working as a morning commuter train from Rhymney into Cardiff Central, this four coach train stabled all day at Canton before returning in the evening. It operated Mondays to Fridays. After a few false starts which included power by a privately owned Class 33, a Class 50 and numerous 47s (including ex-Scottish 47/7s), the line settled down to regular Class 37 haulage and that is how it remained for more than a decade. From two trains on a weekday, the service blossomed into six trains (three locos) on a weekday and a full loco-hauled hourly service on a Saturday. By the end of 2005, the line had gained cult status and from some obsure Welsh branch line that had a two-hourly 'Bubble' car service only 20 years earlier, this 23-mile line became the last in the country to run daytime diesel hauled passenger trains anywhere in Britain. 37420 'The Scottish Hosteller' in the early days runs off the viaduct at Pontlottyn on the last stretch of the journey to Rhymney. Note the huge red dragon on the headcode box! *(John Griffiths)*

From an original rake of Waterman Railways mark 2Ds, painted in black and cream, came a second rake of Forward Trust Rail (later HSBC-owned) mark 2As painted in blue and cream and named after female staff members (the rake opposite). By late 2001 and into 2002, as services increased, four rakes of four coaches were hired in from the West Coast Railway Company, painted in maroon. These 16 vehicles were mostly air conditioned mark 2s, with a few of the earlier mark 2B and 2C vehicles. All of these had central door locking. Regarding the 37/4s and remarkably, over the years, 30 of the 31-strong fleet worked to Rhymney. The missing loco was 37404 which was allocated on 28th January 1999 but was failed by the driver prior to departure from Canton! The loco had suffered a traction motor flashover and never ran again. Locos like 37402 and 37412 worked for years while others came and went. 37422, pictured earlier in Regional Railways livery, was another machine which made odd appearances. Working mostly in the North West and North Wales in the mid and late 1990s, the loco became a regular on the Rhymney line in September and October 1999 prior to withdrawal. After a prolonged overhaul and a new name 'Cardiff Canton', 37422 returned to the Rhymney line in 2003 and is pictured here just out of Rhymney in a gleaming coat of EWS maroon and gold complete with a rake of (near) matching carriages. Regrettably, the return was short lived as the loco was in and out of service, missing most of 2004 and was withdrawn again at the end of that year. *(John Griffiths)*

Above: The introduction of Voyager DMUs caused a huge cascade of quality refurbished rolling stock, some of which ended up on the Rhymney line. Now supplied by Riviera Trains, these ex-Cross Country mark 2Fs in Inter City and Virgin livery became common from July 2003 onwards. 37410 was one of the less common Rhymney locos and only worked during summer 2003. Based in Scotland from conversion in 1985, the loco worked a full diagram on this Saturday and is pictured here at Pontlottyn working 2R18, the 10.59 Cardiff to Rhymney. *(Phil Wright)*

Opposite: Looking at some of the more exotic 37s which worked Rhymney services and this is 37796 and 37802. Double heading was exceptionally rare on the Rhymney line but this pairing had come about as a result of the Barry Transport Festival on Sunday 6th June 1999. Locos 37796, 37802, 50031 and D444 (50044) worked two special trains from Rhymney to Barry Town, including two trips to Cwm Bargoed before a return to Rhymney. Still coupled, the 37s worked 2V07, the 07.23 Rhymney to Radyr on the Monday morning, seen here reversing into the platform at Rhymney. *(Nick Meskell collection)*

DOUBLE HEADER

NO HEAT!

Right: Due to failures and shortages, a real mixed bag of no-heat 37s worked Rhymney services over the years. It was easier in the early days, with the stock not requiring an ETS supply and many 37/4s were tied up elsewhere in the UK. If a failure occurred, any spare type 3 could be allocated off Canton. 37678 in de-branded two tone grey stands at Caerphilly on Saturday 26th June 1999. Having worked 2R62, the 21.05 Cardiff to Rhymney on the Friday evening, the loco went on to work five return trips the following day.
(Nick Meskell collection)

Left: Civil Engineers livery at Rhymney on a misty 20th April 1999. Former Scottish stalwart 37264 is seen prior to working 2F42, the 07.41 to Cardiff. This was a brief out and back affair with the loco having worked 2R42, the 17.05 Cardiff to Rhymney the previous evening. Take away the livery and this ex-Eastfield and Inverness based former boiler fitted loco could well be at Oban or Kyle prior to a morning working. In fact, wind the clock back exactly 14 years to the day and 37264 worked 2K02, the 06.55 Inverness to Kyle on 20th April 1985! Thankfully, there is some good news and this fine machine is presently undergoing restoration in Tyseley at the Birmingham Railway Museum.
(Nick Meskell collection)

Left: Loadhaul in the valleys with the mighty 37884 'Gartcosh' on 6th May 1998. The 'Heavyweight' spent a few days on South Wales passenger duties between the 4th and 7th May 1998. Apologies for another image at Rhymney, but it would seem that the photographer was snapping what he rode on and on this particular morning he had this beast on 2F40, the 07.21 to Cardiff. 37884 returned on 2O38, the 16.32 ex-Cardiff that same evening. The Loadhaul livery was well received by photographers. The black and orange was in stark contrast to the green of the valleys! 37884 was based at Immingham when it worked these trains.
(Nick Meskell collection)

Right: Although the timetable changed a bit over the years, one of the morning loco-hauled trains from Rhymney was extended 4.75 miles to Radyr where it ran round and returned empty to Canton. There was never an evening train. Pictured upon arrival at Radyr, this is 37797 on 12th August 1999 having worked 2V07, the 07.23 from Rhymney. This loco enjoyed a three day stint on the Rhymney circuit working this same train on both the 12th and 13th August. Based at Cardiff between 1986 and 1996, the loco was allocated to Toton when it worked here.
(Nick Meskell collection)

In October 1994 when the three former Trainload sectors became separate businesses as Loadhaul, Transrail and Mainline, the UK rail scene was to witness the birth of three new liveries. From the delightful orange and black of Loadhaul and the simple big 'T' on grey for Transrail came the stylish aircraft blue and silver colours of Mainline. Initially Mainline applied a simple transfer over the existing sub-sector branding which later developed into a full blown corporate livery of its own and, when clean and new, was absolutely stunning. 58050 was first, launched in October 1995 and repaints to Classes 08, 09, 31, 37, 60 and 73 all followed. 31407 was unique as far as the 31s are concerned, but of the 37s, 23 locos received these colours between 1994 and 1996. 37198 was painted at Stewarts Lane depot in August 1995. The loco was based there, working in the EWDB pool at this time. Four years on, looking a little beaten in what was now an obsolete livery and based at Toton in the WKBN pool, this machine was required for passenger service and is seen here leaving Cardiff with 2R40, the 16.46 to Rhymney. (16th August). The loco had found its way on to the Rhymney circuit, having worked a special from Rhymney to Tenby and back on the previous day. It then worked commuter services for four days! Looking at records from summer 1999 and this loco put in a few appearances on South Wales passenger trains, enjoying a full day on the Rhymney branch on Saturday 26th June, odd weekday journeys also in June and a few outings on the Bristol/Weymouth/Cardiff diagram in July and August. Today 37198 is alive and well, owned by Bedale Railway Engines Limited, fully restored in a coat of BR blue and working on the Dartmoor Railway. *(Jim Ramsay)*

The introduction of air conditioned stock with central door locking posed a few problems for the Rhymney line. Of course, these carriages were safer, newer and more comfortable for passengers but they really had to be hauled by 37/4s. If a non-ETS fitted loco substituted, it really should have been just for one journey to avoid stuffy coaches and/or central door lock failure. One such substitution was on Saturday 10th April 2004 when 37203 was drafted in for a full days work. From Cardiff at 08.59, the loco ran five trips to Rhymney, stabled on the Sunday and then worked another five round trips on the Monday! (Easter Monday). Finishing at Rhymney on Monday night, the adventure ended with the 07.19 to Cardiff and oblivion on the Tuesday morning. 37203 (note the different nose end number size) had stepped in following the failure of 37402. In turn, 37203s place was taken by 37406 on the Tuesday. Pictured at Caerphilly, this was 2F42, the 16.15 Rhymney to Cardiff on the Saturday afternoon. *(Pete Rogers)*

RHYMNEY REGULARS

During the final months of full time loco-hauled trains on the Rhymney branch a small pool of regular 37s were employed. With virtually no booked passenger or freight (except the Caledonian Sleeper in Scotland), EWS basically gathered the best of the surviving locos and transferred them to Cardiff and later, Margam. A trio of machines, 37405, 37408 'Loch Rannoch' and 37411 'The Scottish Railway Preservation Society' arrived in Wales on the back of a bizarre passenger diagram from 2003/2004. Using two locos (top and tail) on four coaches on a weekday diagram which started out as an empty stock move from Healey Mills to Knaresborough. From Knaresborough they worked a commuter service to Leeds, then the 09.47 to Carlisle, returning with 13.33 Carlisle to Leeds, 17.43 to Knaresborough and ecs back to Healey Mills. When this service finished in September 2004, the three locos concerned headed for Wales and along with 37419 and 37425, became devotees of the Rhymney line. The image above probably describes the final years of the Rhymney line to perfection: Maroon and gold loco, red and white stock and a green green valley! *(Phil Wright)*

With an already illustrious history of passenger work in Scotland and North Wales, 37402 'Bont Y Bermo' was one of the most regular performers on the Rhymney line. After a move to Canton in November 2001, this loco worked hundreds of journeys until withdrawal in December 2004. It even acquired its very own livery - seen here at Tir-phil on a misty 4th December 2004 heading to Cardiff. *(Phil Wright)*

'HERITAGE' REPAINTS

With the end of loco-hauled services planned for December 2005, Arriva Trains Wales funded two special repaints. 37411 (now de-named) went into original BR green with a small yellow warning panel while 37425 above was out shopped in the delightful Large Logo livery. Having already gained cult worship, these two repaints brought even more enthusiasts to the lineside and on to the trains and with an hourly service and three locos in operation, there was a virtual Class 37 gala every Saturday! In total, there were 13 departures from Rhymney between 07.05 and 20.20. Oddly, diagram 3 finished the day at Cardiff which meant a Sunday empty stock move from Canton to Rhymney thus balancing the three sets for Monday morning. Although only an ecs move, loco-hauled trains of any kind were very rare on Sundays. Looking fantastic in any weather, 37425 rounds the curve at Ystrad Mynach heading for Cardiff in summer 2005. *(Phil Wright)*

Taken at Pontlottyn, in the same location as 37410 on page 46 and this is 37411 among some incredible autumn colours. Pictured on Saturday 19th November 2005, this was 2R14, the 09.59 Cardiff to Rhymney. Following the demise of the aforementioned Leeds - Carlisle service, the Arriva liveried carriages used on that run ended up in the Valleys, providing yet more colourful train and loco combinations. It got worse when some of these carriages were mixed with the ex-Virgin red stock and with a Large logo, maroon or even a BR green locomotive, the possibilities were endless. 37411 shows off a green and turquoise mix to full effect. Just nine days after this photo was taken both 37411 and 37425 were named in a twin ceremony at Caerphilly Station. Having worked all summer in their heritage liveries without nameplates, it was somewhat odd that they should be named just 12 days before the service was due to finish. Perhaps there was a hidden agenda! *(Pete Rogers)*

Just like the passing of the Deltics, 40s, Peaks and 50s before them, the final day of full loco haulage on the Rhymney line created a buzz of excitement with many wellwishers and enthusiasts out and about for the final time. It was Saturday 10th December 2005, a cold yet dry winter day and 37405, 37411 and 37419 were allocated. 37405 was first out from Rhymney, with the 07.05 to Cardiff, 37419 worked the 08.01 and 37411 did diagram 3, kicking off with 2F14, the 09.13 to Cardiff. On the previous Sunday (4th) there was a farewell gala featuring 33207, 37411, 37419, 37425, 47854, 50031 and 50049 but for all intents and purposes, this Saturday was the last 'real' day. 37411 is pictured at Cardiff Central prior to working 2R42, the 16.59 to Rhymney. Looking fantastic with a spotlessly clean three piece miniature snowplough and the proud 'Castell Caerffili / Caerphilly Castle' nameplates, 37411 really looks the part. In fact, take away the modern fittings and this is pretty much what D6990 would have looked like 41 years earlier in June 1965, when it was allocated brand new to Canton and it may well have stood here on some lengthy coal train! *(Phil Wright)*

Such was the emotion and passion for the 37s in South Wales somebody went to the effort of attaching two wreaths to the front of 37419 prior to working the last train. This stunning image shows 37419 at Caerphilly on that last working, 2F70, the 20.20 Rhymney to Cardiff on 10th December 2005. The diagrams were slightly altered on this last day, so that all three sets finished at Canton. Prior to this, 37419 had had the honour of working the last northbound train, 2R54, the 19.05 ex-Cardiff. It was somewhat ironic that 37419 worked the last trains. This loco was actually surplus at the back end of 2004 and switched off. However, due to the untimely demise of 37408 in August 2005, it was resurrected and worked regularly for the final five months. The words 'farewell' and 'last ever' are overused in today's railways and although nobody would criticise Arriva Trains Wales for their efforts in providing a good send off, the saying goes that you can't kill the undead and no sooner had the 'last trains' run, 37s returned to the Rhymney line in 2006. It may only be one diagram Mondays to Fridays, for which 37425 has provided the power but at the time of writing the South Wales Class 37 is alive and well and growling its way to Rhymney! *(Phil Wright)*

DIESEL-HAULED PASSENGER TRAINS 7 INTO THE VALLEY...

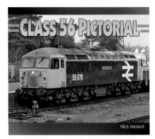

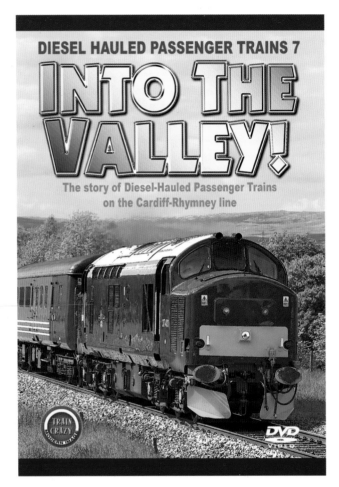

**Join Train Crazy as we go.....
INTO THE VALLEY!**

Nobody ever imagined that the Cardiff - Rhymney line would have become the last location in the country to operate daytime diesel hauled passenger trains. With the painting of 37411 into BR green and 37425 into Large Logo, this 23 mile branch line gained cult status in the final months of 2005.

INTO THE VALLEY tells the story of diesel hauled passenger trains, from the early years with a green 33 and a Large Logo 50, right through to 37 operation and the farewell gala day.
Train Crazy tells the story of Diesel Hauled Passenger Trains on the Cardiff - Rhymney line including:

- **The early years with 33208, 50031 and no-heat 37s**
- The unofficial diesel gala from March 2000 with seven locos in action
- **Year by year changes, new liveries, new coaches and extra trains**
- The day 56115 worked from Rhymney - exclusive unseen footage
- **Summer 2005 with 37411 in green and 37425 in Large Logo**
- The gala day from December 2005 featuring Class 33, 37, 47 and 50 locos

105 Minutes VHS & DVD £14.95   *(Code: TC41)*

Please contact us for full details of all of these items and a copy of our free catalogue.

Post: Train Crazy, FREEPOST, Blackpool. FY4 1BR.
Telephone & Fax: 01253 346005
email: admin@train-crazy.co.uk
website: www.train-crazy.co.uk

***For full details of all these titles,
please contact us or visit our website:***

www.train-crazy.co.uk
Many other titles available.